MW00768902

On

Becoming

the Person

You Want

to Be

Henry E. Roberts

Ardara House, Publishers
1500 East Johnson Avenue, Suite 123
Pensacola, Florida 32514
850 479 7962

On
Becoming
the Person
You Want
to Be

© 1997 by Henry E. Roberts. All rights reserved. No part of this work may be reproduced or transmitted in any form or by any means, electronic or mechanical, including photocopying and recording, or by any information storage or retrieval system except as may be expressly permitted by the 1976 Copyright Act or in writing from the author. Requests for permission should be addressed in writing to Dr. Henry E. Roberts, 6 East Wright Street, Pensacola, Florida, 32501.

In not using capital letters for pronouns that refer to the deity, the editors have followed the style utilized in the King James Version and the New Revised Standard Version of the scriptures. We have set in italics direct quotations from the Old Testament and the New Testament.

Unless noted, the New Revised Standard Version has been used in biblical quotations. Abbreviations for other references include TM for Eugene Peterson's THE MESSAGE, KJV for the King James Version, and TJB for The Jerusalem Bible.

Library of Congress Catalog Card Number: 97-73790
ISBN: 1-888676-04-3

> To my father
> James Henry Roberts
> January 17, 1911—March 14, 1997

I will forever be grateful that God gave me a wonderful mother and father, the most blessed of beginnings.

This year my father died. He worked hard all the eighty-six years of his life. He served the church and the communities in which he lived. He loved his family and especially my mother, with whom he shared the marriage covenant for sixty-one years. After she was crippled by a stroke in 1988, he devoted himself to taking care of her.

I have dedicated this book to my father, who, though no longer among us, is alive today. He lives in my heart and mind and actions. He lives in my brother Jimmy's drive to put first things first and in Jimmy's caring, protecting ways. My father lives in heaven, that mysterious experience of being in the close presence of God, who gave him to the world eighty-six years ago. He lives beyond what yet is. He lives beyond—beyond pain, beyond suffering, beyond struggle, beyond sickness and beyond death.

Acknowledgements

For the influence he exerted in the development of my understanding of how we experience the grace of God and the abundant life which is offered to us all, I want to acknowledge my indebtedness to Dr. Robert Wingard, professor at Birmingham-Southern College, who died this year. Bob opened to me and to many the writings of the Apostle Paul by making theological insights clear and contemporary.

For their ability to transform my sketchy ideas and disjointed phrases into understandable sentences and meaningful paragraphs, I want to acknowledge my indebtedness to Pat Brinson, who once again has proven herself to be an invaluable editor, and to George Baskin, my publisher.

And for seasoned counsel, unswerving loyalty, abiding love, and compassionate understanding, I want to again say thank you to my wife Jane, with whom I have shared many ventures and adventures over the past thirty-five years. We have been through many transitions. Having her beside me, always supportive in our ministry and quietly suggesting that I keep Jesus Christ in the forefront of my life and sermons, continues to keep me focused and to strengthen me each day.

Foreword

Over the years in my pastoral ministry many persons in counseling sessions have said in varied ways, "If I could only start over again. If only there really were 'a land of beginning again.'" In some ways this book is a positive response to their searching questions and is given in hope that the reader will discover or perhaps rediscover the abundant life offered by God through Christ.

Stephen R. Covey has said in one of his seminar manuals, "If we live out of our memory, we're tied to the past and to that which is finite. When we live out of our imagination, we're tied to that which is infinite." The question of "Where do I start to become the person I want to be?" can quickly be answered with my response: Right where you are! Don't delay. Seize the moment today and make an inner resolve to move from decision to action, from desire to reality, from memory to imagination.

Pensacola, Florida
September, 1997

Table of Contents

Begin with the end in mind.

Stephen Covey

On Becoming
the Person
You Want to Be

"Today I looked into my wife's sorrowing eyes and saw the reflection of who I have become. I don't like what I saw. I'm here to change, but I don't know where to start. *I need help!*"

These desperate words came from a man leaning toward me from the chair on the other side of my desk. After years of cheating and compromise, his life was in shambles. As my mind wrapped itself around the challenge before me, my heart felt glad to realize that those are the words and the spirit which God is waiting for. The person who is dissatisfied with himself can change.

In the rural South several years ago there was an irritating, over-zealous, under-educated minister who served a small church. Several members of his congregation circulated a petition declaring him unfit to serve the church. He heard about the petition and spent several days tracking it down. When at last the pastor was able to get his hands on the petition, he promptly signed it! Many Christians know exactly how he felt. He was totally dissatisfied with his life, with his service to God. The positive thing is that he recognized where he was in his growth and maturation as a person.

My friend with the broken pieces of his life in his hand also realized who he had become. Actually, he sounded just like I imagine Adam sounded when, in the marvelous story from Genesis, he saw himself naked before God and realized who he had become. Adam said to God, "I was afraid and hid myself."

He sounded like King David, when Nathan came to him and stripped him raw with the revelation of what David had done to Uriah and Bathsheba. He said in that devastating moment of self-understanding, "I have sinned against the Lord."

He sounded like the Apostle Peter when, in the hours before the crucifixion, Peter heard the cock crow for the second time and wept.

In the way of individuals throughout time, my distraught friend said: "I looked into the eyes of my wife and didn't like what I saw reflected there. How can I become the person I want to be?"

If you are asking in your heart "Where do I start to become the person I want to be?" your good intentions may be lost in the helpless feeling of being directionless.

Even Augustine, of the city of Hippo in North Africa, revered now for centuries as a saint, had these feelings. In his *Confessions*, he

tells us everything—his jealousies in infancy, his thieving as a boy, his stormy relationship with his overbearing mother [. . .] his years of philandering, his breakdowns, his shameful love for an unnamed peasant woman, whom he finally sends away. His self-loathing is as modern as that of a character in Camus or Beckett—and as concrete: "I carried inside me a cut and bleeding soul, and how to get rid of it I just didn't know. I sought every plea-sure—the countryside, sports, fooling around, the peace of a garden, friends and good company, sex, reading. My soul floundered in the void—and came back upon me. For where could my heart flee from my heart? Where could I escape from myself?"[1]

If, like Augustine, you are floundering and looking for a sense of purpose, resolve to make a new beginning. You can have the assurance that you are in the center of the will of God for your life! You can become the kind of person you want to be! Today is the day to begin.

Here are three suggestions to get you going. Each is important and all are inter-related.

**Realize God is reaching for you
as you reach for God**

Throughout the pages of the Holy Scriptures, we are told that God is reaching for, is seeking a relationship with, humankind. It is not that we are so valuable but that God is so good.

The Apostle Paul writes time after time of God's saving grace. Grace is the key to everything else he understood about God's work accomplished in Jesus. He wrote *But God, . . . even when we were dead through our trespasses, made us alive together with Christ . . . . For by grace have you been saved, through faith, and this is not of your own doing, it is the gift of God* (Ephesians 2:5,8). This is his theme again and again: it was not that anyone at any time deserved what God did. It was that God was communicating something about his nature and his ways to all of humankind for all time. He was communicating his amazing grace. In spite of your sin, not because of your righteousness, you have been saved.

That is our understanding of the cross of Jesus. On the cross, God did something for us that we could not do for ourselves. *For God so loved the world that he gave his only son* (John 3:16). Peter said of the early Christians, "Once you were nobody but now you are somebody" (paraphrase of I Peter 2:10).

If you are a major league baseball fan, you may recall that for a few weeks during the spring of 1995 there was a strike of both the major and minor league players. They were negotiating for more money and so the owners, determined to start the season, threw open the gates and hired anyone who had a glove and could swing a bat. The million-dollar arms stayed at home and the cadillac bats were in the rack. The players were has-beens or fellows who one day were coaching little league and the next were wearing a major league uniform.

The games weren't fancy. There were very few home runs. One manager said his pitchers threw the ball so slow that the radar gun couldn't clock them. The players huffed and puffed more than the Little Engine that thought it could.

But the players had great fun and those who watched the games did, too. The players were there because they loved the game, not because they were great or thought they would be there forever or deserved to be there or were paid big bucks. The experience was special because these guys knew they were living a life they didn't expect. They weren't picked because they were the best; they were picked because they were willing. And they knew it. When the coach asked for a volunteer to shag flies, a dozen hands went up. These fellows arrived before the park was open, greasing their gloves and cleaning their cleats. They stayed late to help the grounds crew clean the field. They thanked the attendants for washing their uniforms. They thanked the fans for paying to come out to the park to watch them play. These guys didn't see themselves as a blessing to baseball, rather baseball as a blessing to them. They didn't demand more play time; they were thrilled to play at all. They didn't expect luxury; they were surprised by it.

Shouldn't we feel this way? Aren't we a lot like the pickup players? Look at us. Certainly not because of our skills or abilities or past records, our names are on the greatest roster of history. God's grace has placed us on a dream team beyond imagination. Our past is pardoned, and our future is secure. We have only to claim the knowledge that God draws us unto Himself.

This open embrace can be felt in unexpected places if only we are aware. In *Mentoring, The Ministry of Spiritual Kinship,* Catholic theologian Edward Sellner tells the story of finding his two-year-old son playing in his study:

As I watched silently for a few moments unobserved, Daniel turned his attention from the toy fire truck he was holding to a tiny painted picture of Jesus located on a small table near the window. Without a moment's thought he suddenly leaned over and gave the picture a gentle kiss. Then, just as quickly, he returned to the fire truck and his play.

His simple act, done so spontaneously, took me by surprise. I knew that he had never seen me kiss the picture. I knew too that he was not fully aware of whose picture was portrayed there, or the rich history of spirituality it contained. And yet he had kissed the picture so naturally in the midst of what he enjoyed doing that I wondered what was behind his gesture of love and respect.

"Daniel," I said, interrupting his play, "who is that man whose picture you just kissed?" Without hesitating he replied, "He's a good guy, Dad, a good guy . . . ." [2]

Amazing! In the face painted by an Eastern Orthodox artist long ago the child perceived the essence of the man Jesus. Like the boy, we don't know God fully, but the mystery surrounding God is cut through by our human experiences of love and goodness.

Sellner writes of the conscious and unconscious levels on which we are drawn to the reality of God:

> This is what spirituality is about: being drawn to the sacred through the icons of our lives, that is, the images, symbols, rituals, experiences and, most important, the relationships that transform us by their love. It is about developing a relationship with God, the Holy One and source of goodness, who may seem very distant and unknowable at times, and yet is present to us as friend, often in unexpected and seemingly hopeless situations.

When we profess our faith in Christ we enter a unique and close relationship with God. We become children of God, members of the family of God. Then, as time passes, many of us become focused on our careers, on important affairs of business, even on our families, and let that most important of relationships languish.

In the Service of Baptism in the United Methodist Church each one of us is asked, "Do you confess Jesus Christ as your Savior and put your whole trust in his grace?" A positive answer to this question is the place to start to become the person you want to be.

**Realize with humility
that you are what you are
and have what you have
because of the goodness of God**

The Old Testament story of Micah was written about a time when God's people had forgotten what it means to walk with God. In their arrogance the people had forgotten that they were blessed. They did not remember God's acts of mercy or their deliverance from slavery and their entrance into the Promised Land. God's people had tried to substitute animal sacrifices for that life of justice, loyalty and humility, which God expects. They had forgotten their covenant with God. To remind them of their arrogance and call them to humility Micah gave them—and us—a powerful word:

"With what shall I come before the Lord,
  and bow myself before God on high?
Shall I come before him with burnt offerings,
  with calves a year old?
Will the Lord be pleased with thousands of rams,
  with ten thousands of rivers of oil?
Shall I give my first born for my transgression,
  the fruit of my body for the sin of my soul?"
He has told you, o mortal, what is good;
  and what does the Lord require of you
but to do justice, and to love kindness,
  and to walk humbly with your God?

                                              Micah 6:6-8

Remember this. God is always maintaining his part of the relationship. When you let your end go, you begin to think he is lost to you. In reality, the relationship will reconnect when you focus on God. Realize what God has done for you: he has created you, given you gifts in abundance, opened to you the door of salvation through Jesus Christ, taught you what is of value and how to live life at its best. God is always waiting for you to acknowledge his presence and to reach out to him.

During a Vacation Bible School session with the children, I asked them what part of the worship service they like best. One very bright child raised his hand and said, "The benediction."

Jokingly, I said something like "I guess that means we are at the end of the service and can go home."

"No," he said, "it is because that is when you bless us. When you tell us that God will be with us all the time."

Although a little embarrassed at my joking response, I also felt very proud. I realized that this child had pinpointed another juncture where we can begin to become who we want to be. And where we can begin it anew every week. When we accept that God will be with us, we can begin becoming who we want to be.

One of the lessons in the *Disciple* Bible Study, which many people across the country are using as a guide to in-depth study, begins with a statement of our problem: "We want to feel important, to be in charge, to make a name for ourselves. We don't need anyone else. We'll create our own meaning and take credit for it. Then we cannot understand why we feel alienated from others."

Jesus told a story to some who were complacently pleased with themselves over their moral performance and looked down their noses at the common people:

> *"Two men went up to the temple to pray, one a Pharisee, the other a tax man. The Pharisee posed and prayed like this: 'Oh, God, I thank you that I am not like other people—robbers, crooks, adulterers, or, heaven forbid, like this tax man. I fast twice a week and tithe on all my income.'*
>
> *"Meanwhile the tax man, slumped in the shadows, his face in his hands, not daring to look up, said, 'God, give mercy. Forgive me, a sinner.'"* Luke 18:9-13 TM

If we place ourselves in this revealing story, we may be more like the Pharisee than we are the tax collector, the humble sinner. This scripture illustrates the truth of how we must approach God. If we develop a persistent yet humble spirit, we are on the road to becoming the kind of person we dream about becoming.

Jesus affirmed it in his parable:

"This tax man, not the other, went home made right with God. If you walk around with your nose in the air, you're going to end up flat on your face, but if you're content to be simply yourself, you will become more than yourself."

Luke 18:14 TM

Humility is a tricky kind of concept, however. Golda Meir, the woman who was a world leader and Prime Minister of Israel during critical times, once said to a visiting diplomat, "Don't be so humble; you're not that great."

C. S. Lewis wrote a book, *The Screwtape Letters*, which contained humorous but highly instructive letters from the Devil to his nephew Wormwood, who had been assigned to "take care" of a certain human person. In one of those letters Lewis has the Devil coach Wormwood in the way to rid that person of humility.

Your patient has become humble; have you drawn his attention to the fact? All virtues are less formidable to us once the man is aware that he has them, but this is specially true of humility. Catch him at the moment when he is really poor in spirit and smuggle into his mind the gratification reflection, "By jove! I'm being humble," and almost immediately pride—pride at his own humility—will appear. If he awakes to the danger and tries to smother this new form of pride, make him proud of his attempt—and so on, through as many stages as you please. But don't try this too long, for fear you awake his sense of humor and proportion, in which case he will merely laugh at you and go to bed.[3]

In his epistle "to the twelve tribes scattered to Kingdom Come," James offers this advice: *Get down on your knees before the Master; it's the only way you'll get on your feet* (James 4:10 TM).

Paul gave good advice, as well:

Think of yourselves the way Christ Jesus thought of himself. He had equal status with God but didn't think so much of himself that he had to cling to the advantages of that status no matter what. Not at all. When the time came, he set aside the privileges of deity and took on the status of a slave, became human! Having become human, he stayed human. It was an incredibly humbling process. He didn't claim special privileges. Instead, he lived a selfless, obedient life and then died a selfless, obedient death—and the worst kind of death at that: a crucifixion.

Philippians 2:5-8 TM

Jesus set the example on many occasions. During one of the last events before his death he demonstrated his servant role by washing the feet of his disciples. "Humility," wrote Mother Teresa, "is nothing but truth . . . . If you are humble, nothing will touch you, neither praise nor disgrace, because you know what you are."[4] Like Jesus, Mother Teresa taught us that we stand tallest when we stoop to serve.

Tell me this, honestly. If you are sick at heart because you don't like who you are, have you tried serving with humility? Without seeking credit or fame for it? Without getting your name in the newspaper? When you wrap yourself in the mantle of humility and step into the role of servant, you can start to become the person you want to be.

Start in small ways to become a servant

Begin at home. Be a different person around

the house. Pick up your own trash, be easier to live with, carry your share of the load, do your homework, be thoughtful of the others, wash the car, prepare the meal, set an example, smile!

William James wrote:

> I am done with great things and big things, with great institutions and big successes, and I am for those tiny, invisible, molecular forces that work from individual to individual, creeping through the crannies of the world like so many soft rootlets, or like the capillary oozing of water, but which, given time, will rend the hardest monuments of human pride.

The importance of the 1996 Million Man March on Washington will ultimately be measured only by the small changes in the lives of the men who marched. The men interviewed said, "I'm going to be a better father" or "I'm going to be a better worker" or "I'm going to be more dependable." Their keeping of these vows is what will make a difference after all of the speeches are forgotten and all the controversy is quieted.

The organization called Promise Keepers was

formed by a former University of Colorado football coach to help men be responsible, faithful, promise-keeping men. They've packed stadiums all across the country with their meetings. If it works, then I say "Great!" We already know that the macho "I'll-do-what-I-damn-well-please, you-take-care-of-the-kids" attitude isn't working, and the children are suffering. So I say to the men, if you want to become the person you've dreamed of being, start with the small things: change the diapers, rake the yard, sit in church with your child, pray for your wife and children!

To all I say, if you are not happy with your life and want to start again, then start small, by being a good parent, a good student, a good worker, a good neighbor, a good practitioner of Jesus' teachings. I know a couple who have a busy dental practice. They schedule their patients on a split schedule so that they can handle their patients, maintain their family responsibilities, and do the other things that are important to them, such as teaching in the Vacation Bible School. They didn't start by organizing a huge public event. They started small. They arranged their lives in order to commit to the important "small" things.

In the church where I am pastor we have many individuals who seek no recognition for their servant roles. There's the man whom I call on holidays or at the crack of dawn on summer Sundays when the sanctuary air conditioning doesn't work. There are the folks who put together wheelchairs for needy children in Jamaica, those who haul and unload food for the food bank, those who drive the sick to doctors' appointments or support those with troubled minds and hearts. All of these persons work cheerfully and humbly in a servant role without recognition.

The truth of the story in the scriptures about the humble spirit of the tax man is that you can change, that you can become who you want to be. I don't think you will want to become like the Pharisee; neither will you want to become like the tax man. **Why don't you simply be the *you* that waits to be! God must have liked the potential you, for he formed you.**

God is reaching out to you, even as you yearn

toward God. He has given you all that is good within you, and offers you strength to change whatever needs to be changed. Reach out to God, with the knowledge that you can't succeed alone. Then start in small ways to live a servant life, and you can start to become the person you want to be, the person God intended you to be.

You are what you have been becoming! And you will be the same tomorrow if you don't will yourself to start the new journey right now. The difference is that it will be much more difficult to start the change tomorrow than it is today. Wherever you are as you read this, you can walk out different from what you were when you walked in.

As a deer longs for flowing streams,
so my soul longs for you,
O God.
My soul thirsts for God,
for the living God.

Psalm 42:1,2

Drink of the Living Water

Built into our physical nature is the desire for water to satisfy our thirst. The fact is that we have to have certain amounts of air, food, and water to maintain our bodies. We need to consume at least six eight-ounce glasses of water every day to keep adequately hydrated. When we exercise or experience high stress, our bodies use a lot of fluids that we sometimes fail to replace. If this happens, our bodies become dehydrated.

This is our physical condition. But it also describes our emotional, mental, and spiritual lives. We hunger and thirst for a better self. We hunger and thirst for a secure relationship with the Creator.

What are your mind and heart thirsting for

today? Fame and recognition, your name in lights over the theater or on the sports pages? Money and a Mercedes Benz? Endless sensual pleasure? Good luck! Maybe you'll find all of that! But I can tell you, from universal experience: when you get all of that, you'll still be thirsty.

Many persons live lives which are characterized by restlessness and an almost insatiable desire for *MORE*. One way we start becoming the persons we want to be, with our emotional and spiritual needs fully met, is to drink of the Living Water which Jesus describes in the story from John's Gospel.

> *He came into Sychar, a Samaritan village that bordered the field Jacob had given his son Joseph. Jacob's well was still there. Jesus, worn out by the trip, sat down at the well. It was noon.*
>
> *A woman, a Samaritan, came to draw water. Jesus said, "Would you give me a drink of water?" . . . .*
>
> *The Samaritan woman, taken aback, asked, "How come you, a Jew, are asking me, a Samaritan woman, for a drink?" (Jews in those days wouldn't be caught dead talking to Samaritans.)*
>
> *Jesus answered, "If you knew the generosity of God and who I am, you would be*

asking me for a drink, and I would give you fresh, living water."

The woman said, "Sir, you don't even have a bucket to draw with, and this well is deep. So how are you going to get this 'living water'? Are you a better man than our ancestor Jacob, who dug this well and drank from it, he and his sons and livestock, and passed it down to us?"

Jesus said, "Everyone who drinks this water will get thirsty again and again. Anyone who drinks the water I give will never thirst—not ever. The water I give will be an artesian spring within, gushing fountains of endless life."

The woman said, "Sir, give me this water so I won't ever get thirsty, won't ever have to come back to this well again!"

John 4:5-15 TM

Water, as a symbol of the satisfaction of man's greatest continuing need, is a frequent metaphor in the scriptures. Living water is understood to mean running water, as opposed to rain water, caught and imprisoned in containers of one sort or another.

Recently, when friends from a mining town on the western edge of Siberia came to our city, it was their very first exposure to western abundance.

They went to visit a supermarket and were astounded by a fascinating world containing products they had never known existed.

They found on the beverage shelves Mountain Blackberry water, Country Raspberry water, Summer Strawberry water, Orchard Peach water, Wild Cherry water, sparkling water, Perrier natural water, Clearly Canadian water, and Whiterock Tonic water. They saw sixty-eight choices of carbonated drinks and twice that many types of alcoholic drinks, to say nothing about fruit and vegetable juices and several types of milk.

The woman at the well in Samaria would have been as astonished as our Russian friends if she had to go to the well of a modern supermarket to get her water. Everything is attractively packaged to claim our attention and titillate our desires. In the world's marketplace there are found many products to help us satisfy our thirsts and hungers.

Greater even than our physical need for fluids, however, is the spiritual need to satisfy the thirst for a better self. The big issues of our lives are the driving inner forces: to be loved, to feel secure, to be appreciated, to belong, to improve, to be more than we ever imagined we could become. These inner drives can be satisfied only by what Jesus calls "the living water." He said, *Anyone who drinks the water I give will never thirst—not ever. The water I give will be an artesian spring within, gushing fountains of endless life.*

What a remarkable metaphor! Living water! Gushing fountains of endless life! Jesus explains that he refers to a spiritual gift, a spontaneous energy of unfailing interior grace.

In the fourth century Augustine of Hippo, wrote in his *Confessions*, "Thou hast made us for thyself, O Lord, and our hearts are restless until they find rest in thee." In the twentieth century, sixteen hundred years later, Sundar Singh wrote from India, "In comparison with this big world, the human heart is only a small thing. Though the world is so large, it is utterly unable to satisfy this tiny heart. The ever-growing soul and its capacity can be satisfied only in the infinite God. As water is restless until it reaches its level, so the soul has not peace until it rests in God."

Were Augustine and Singh saying that such *rest* in our relationship with God means that we will simply fixate there and, like zombies, sort of quit living? If so, why would St. Paul write about running the race?

I can relate Paul's message to Augustine's in a very personal way. A good friend said to me recently that the only thing worse than running is a runner who is always talking about running. He was pulling my chain because I am a runner. At the Run for Missions, which is a 5K race sponsored by the church where I serve, a reporter who knew that my legs had been injured in an accident asked me why I wanted to run again. After about two-and-a-half miles into the race I was asking myself that same question! Why did I want to make myself go through that kind of torture again? Let me see if I can tell you and relate it to what St. Augustine wrote about finding rest in God. There is no contradiction.

There is more to life than we have yet experienced. More places to see, more people to meet, more thoughts to think about, more of the mysteries of God to ponder over, so much more. You cannot live always in your comfort zone and grow in God's grace. Most scientists tell us that we use about forty percent of our brain's capacity. Another sixty percent sits there, dormant. Some folks are not even using forty percent! There is so much more to life than we have yet experienced, and unless we push our comfort zones back, we may never experience growth. So you set a benchmark, a high point, and then exceed it and set another one. There is no growth in grace in sitting around in your own comfort zone.

So, this year you want to learn more about living the Christian life than you learned last year. You want to read more books than you read last year. You want to give away more of your money than you gave away last year. You want to read more of the Bible and pray more than you did last year. You want to acknowledge where you have fallen short.

Our desires are satisfied, our thirsts are quenched, and we begin to become the persons we want to be when we enter into a right relationship with God and dwell there. When we hear and appropriate for ourselves the words of eternal life, the living water, they become a self-renewing force, constantly ensuring fellowship with Jesus Christ, whom to know is life eternal.

We claim this thirst-quenching drink, this living water, in several ways, but a very basic one is by the confession of our sin.

Several years ago Karl Menninger dealt harshly with therapists and social scientists who sought to rationalize away all evil human behavior by saying that such behavior is merely the result of unfavorable social conditions. In his book *Whatever Became of Sin* Menninger reserved his harshest rebuke for the liberal religious establishment, which had been telling people that there is no such thing as sin. Such an attitude had encouraged an *I'm O.K., You're O.K.* society. What had previously been described as sin, Menninger said, was increasingly being dismissed as "an alternate lifestyle." God had been reduced to a kindly, all-affirming, all-accepting, indulgent therapist who blesses everything and damns nothing. Menninger pointed out correctly that this concept has not been helpful. In our world many are judgmental, unfaithful, cruel, racist, and prejudiced. These behaviors, along with lying, stealing, and a host of others, can only be called *sin*, and it is past time to admit it.

We have done wrong and the Creator God is not pleased. I do not always serve my congregation best by going easy on God's judgment, even though I have a difficult time dealing with a judgmental attitude toward people and life situations which are foreign to my experience. But until we face the truth, we can never be free.

In the movie *Dead Men Walking* the nun affirms the scripture passage "*. . . and you will know the truth, and the truth will make you free*" (John 8:32). The young man condemned to execution is set free spiritually only when he stops blaming everybody else and faces the truth that he did, in fact, commit rape and murder.

We are set free from our insatiable desires, we start becoming the persons we want to be, only when we confess and acknowledge our sin and turn to God.

Let's face it. In some respects living water doesn't have a very long shelf life. I'm fully aware that Jesus said ". . . *shall never thirst.*" But in fact, just as we have to make a weekly trip to the grocery store for some items, we also have to revisit the presence of God. We need to confess our sins daily in our personal prayers and devotions. Just as the Bible admonishes us to confess our sin, it affirms that God can and will do something about it by giving us the presence of the Holy Spirit in our lives. The Holy Spirit is always available to us.

We claim this living water by recognizing and confessing our sins, by accepting God's grace and putting our whole trust in Christ, and by using the restlessness of our hearts to become the persons we want to be.

May you grow up to be righteous
May you grow up to be true
May you always know the truth
And see the light surrounding you.

Bob Dylan

Choose
Foundational Values

If you would not be forgotten
As soon as you are dead and rotten
Either write things worth reading
Or do things worth the writing.

Benjamin Franklin (1706-1790)

This little bit of doggerel is how Ben Franklin is introduced on the Internet website called *The World of Benjamin Franklin*. The extraordinary Ben Franklin was an educator, writer, philosopher, scientist, inventor, and statesman. He was an active member of the Constitutional Convention. He helped frame the Declaration of Independence. In addition to all of that, the Benjamin Franklin that I knew during the early years of my schooling in Marengo County, Alabama, was a man who was concerned about values and spent a great deal of time making sure his life was built on lasting values.

In *Ben Franklin's Autobiography* (which can be downloaded from the Internet) he has listed some values and virtues which he regularly charted on a grid throughout his life so that he could know if he had his life in order.

- Temperance: Eat not to dullness. Drink not to elevation.
- Silence: Speak not but what may benefit others or yourself. Avoid trifling conversation.
- Order: Let all your things have their places. Let each part of your business have its time.
- Resolution: Resolve to perform what you ought. Perform without fail what you resolve.
- Frugality: Make no expense but to do good to others or yourself; i.e., waste nothing.
- Industry: Lose no time. Be always employed in something useful. Cut off all unnecessary actions.
- Sincerity: Use no hurtful deceit. Think

innocently and justly; and, if you speak, speak accordingly.

❧ Justice: Wrong none by doing injuries or omitting the benefits that are your duty.

❧ Moderation: Avoid extremes. Forbear resenting injuries so much as you think they deserve.

❧ Cleanliness: Tolerate no uncleanness in body, clothes or habitation.

❧ Tranquillity: Be not disturbed at trifles or at accidents common or unavoidable.

❧ Chastity: Rarely use venery but for health or offspring—never to dullness, weakness, or the injury of your own or another's peace or reputation.

❧ Humility: Imitate Jesus and Socrates.

Foundational values are the values from which one builds a foundation for living. Do you agree that these thirteen qualities are foundational values? What would you add to Franklin's list? What would you delete?

Jesus recognized the importance of such

values. When He had finished the long discourse which makes up the Sermon on the Mount, He concluded with this admonition:

> *Everyone then who hears these words of mine and acts on them will be like a wise man who built his house on rock. The rain fell, the floods came, and the winds blew and beat on that house, but it did not fall, because it had been founded on rock. And everyone who hears these words of mine and does not act on them will be like a foolish man who built his house on sand. The rain fell, and the floods came, and the winds blew and beat against that house, and it fell—and great was its fall!* Matthew 7:24-27

We do not understand the way the world works. We do not understand how God allows pain and evil and suffering to continue. If we ruled the world, we say bravely, if we made the rules, there would be a lot less suffering from violence and disease. There would be a lot less suffering from the breaking of marriage relationships, from violent acts of greed. There would be fewer patients in mental hospitals and fewer parents in Bosnia placing flowers on the tiny graves of their children. There would not be any need for teenage gangs, kids desperately looking for identity and acceptance by using violence as a means of getting attention and claiming power.

A certain television ad during the professional football season made me think. It prominently featured a very talented two-sport player and the owner of his football team. The owner says, "If I had ten others like him I could rule the world." It scares me to think that owners with big bucks might rule the world! I can't think of *anybody* I would trust with the job! Except, of course, the One who currently has the job!

Why would I ever think that I could create a better world than God did? God created the world the way it was created for reasons best known to God. I'm not going to change that. Realistically, I know that I can't change the world. I can't change the United States. I can't change Florida or even Pensacola. But I know what I can change.

I remember seeing this statement embedded in the marble floor of Westminster Abbey in London:

When I was young and free and imagination had no limits, I dreamed of changing the world. As I grew older and wiser, I discovered the world would not change, so I shortened my sights somewhat and decided to change only my country. But it, too, seemed immovable.

As I grew into my twilight years, in one last attempt, I settled for changing only my family, those closest to me, but alas, they would have none of it.

And now, as I lie on my deathbed, I suddenly realize: If I had only changed myself first, then by example I would have changed my family.

From their inspiration and encouragement, I would then have been able to better my country and, who knows, I may have even changed the world.

How does one change one's self to ultimately change one's family and the world? I believe that a person begins by choosing foundational values for himself or herself.

These values may differ from culture to culture, from country to country, but most of them are the same. A friend of mine showed me the little notebook in which he had written down a list. These, he said, are the values held by a Muslim schoolmaster, Ramon Hasanov, in the mining town of Satka, Russia, where churches in Northwest Florida have a relationship in common mission. They were eating lunch in the Russian's tiny apartment with Ramon's wife, Irina (who is a Christian believer), their interpreter, and Ramon's two teen-age boys, when the talk shifted to the difference in life in the United States and life in Russia. Gradually, as the level of trust increased, they began to talk about personal things. Ramon spoke of the values he and Irina would like to pass on to their children, and my friend, with Ramon's permission, jotted Ramon's list of values in the notebook:

> Truth
> Respect for others
> Trust
> Working for the common good
> Responsibility
> Patriotism

Are these different from the values on which

you are building your life? What are your values?

I often read to my granddaughter bedtime stories from *The Book of Virtues, A Treasury of Great Moral Stories.* William Bennett's book is organized according to the ten virtues he considers to be foundational: self-discipline, compassion, responsibility, friendship, work, courage, perseverance, honesty, loyalty, faith.[5]

Recently, groups in the community where I live were asked to identify and publicize their values. The Mayor's Task Force identified non-violence, community pride, faith, hope, integrity, justice. The Chamber of Commerce listed responsibility, accountability, excellence/continuous improvement, honesty/truth, quality of life, and integrity. The county school board listed equality, honesty, integrity, patriotism, respect, responsibility. Sacred Heart Hospital identified these core values: respect, quality service, simplicity, advocacy for the poor, inventiveness to infinity. The Council on Ministries at the church where I serve also made a list: respect, faithfulness, trustworthiness, responsibility, fairness, caring.

My guess is that Ramon Hasanov, the Russian Muslim, who is a responsible husband, father, and teacher of children, could subscribe to every foundational values in all these lists, with the possible exception of faith. We don't yet have a way of knowing whether faith plays a significant part in Ramon's life. For seventy years his country has been oppressed by an intolerant government which did its very best to stamp out faith and which believed that tolerance was the enemy of communism.

I often become very concerned when I see evidence in the religious community of intolerance or judgmentalness. Tolerance is one type of conduct which I would add to any list of values that I would recommend. The item on Ramon's list, "respect for others," comes very close to it. "Tolerance" in most dictionaries is "the recognition and respect of others' beliefs, practices, etc., without sharing them; freedom from bigotry or prejudice."

My local newspaper carried an article about a public meeting. I was heartsick to read: "Tonight about 2,300 people will hear that not only is tolerance not necessarily a virtue, but also that it's the greatest enemy of Christianity." The article went on to say that "Tolerance has become the greatest threat to everything that you stand for . . . . It undermines everything you believe in."

When I read further that "the push for tolerance has led Christians away from the 'loving the sinner and hating the sin' concept to 'loving the sinner and praising the sin,'" I knew that someone had completely misunderstood the meaning of tolerance. Believe me, I was delighted and relieved when two of my friends, who had gone to hear this lecturer, told me that the account had unfortunately, and certainly unintentionally, misrepresented what he had to say.

The lack of tolerance becomes intolerance. Intolerance is shouting down the speaker who disagrees with you. Intolerance is the first step to bombing an abortion clinic or shooting a doctor who performs abortions. Intolerance is painting swastikas on a synagogue or throwing paint on a statue of Martin Luther King. Intolerance is cursing and spitting at our Muslim neighbors.

Tolerance is not "loving the sinner and

praising the sin," as the announcement stated. Tolerance is love, fine-tuned, which enables us to live in peace amidst the ambiguities of the world God has created.

Tolerance is loving persons beyond our family and circle of friends.

Tolerance is our Christian missionary Sun Lae Kim, taking a bowl of soup to her Communist neighbor in Moscow.

Tolerance is Mary McMillan, who was our missionary to Japan, giving her coat to a Buddhist student.

Tolerance is Voltaire saying "I disapprove of what you say, but I will defend to the death your right to say it."

Tolerance, in its finest, final form, is Jesus Christ on the cross saying "Father, forgive them, for they know not what they do."

But tolerance is never "praising the sin" or in any way condoning acts of evil.

Tolerance is one of the foundational values of Christianity and of democracy, as well.

It is easy enough for me to advise, "Choose

foundational values." But it is not easy to choose values which will help build the foundation for right living, primarily because we live in a world where foundational values are not popular. Let's face it, we live in a world where what deserves to be treated with great care is often treated as if it were of very little worth. Many of us sacrifice everything for that which has little lasting value and which brings us, ultimately, little pleasure.

With the secular world preaching that the things in life to be most valued are money, power, physical beauty, and pleasure, it is no wonder we have confusion about guiding principles. What each one of us must do is to examine our lives as closely as Benjamin Franklin examined his and decide which values we want in our lives, which principles we want to pass on to our children.

If we want to become the persons we yearn to be, we have to define these principles. Few of us are willing to devote the time and care Ben Franklin used in naming the attributes he would strive for in his life, but we would all benefit from the exercise. You might feel overwhelmed with a list of ten or twelve. Not to worry. Focus on the one you think you need most to develop. Be diligent and record your progress. You'll find yourself coming to be more like the person you want to be!

Dear God, make us free and we shall be free indeed! Free from excessive care and concern about ourselves. Free from fixation with our health. Free from constant worry over money. Free from the fear of the future. Free of anxiety about how others judge us, free of worry about our children and how they will grow up. Remind us, dear God, of that which we so easily forget: your love for us, your loving forgiveness of us and your acceptance of us. Remind us that when we are your captives, we are truly free.

Lord, make us free, and we shall be free indeed. Free us for a greater concern for the needs of others, particularly for the poor, those who have not been blessed with our opportunities, and those who live in danger. Free us for service to the world beyond our family and friends. Show each of us the little things we can do to make life more bearable and the world more lovable for those who have experienced much pain and ugliness in life.

Lord, make us free, and we shall be free indeed, through Christ our Lord. Amen.

Pastoral Prayer

Know That You
Are Called to Be Free

God wills us free,
Man wills us slaves.
I will as God wills,
God's will be done.

(Epitaph on gravestone of John Jack, "A Native of Africa,
who died March 1774, aged about 60 years. Though born in a land
of slavery he was born free.")

Slavery is commonly understood to be the
bondage of an individual to another, who has
complete control and exacts hard labor. Although
persons in the United States are no longer born into
the institution of slavery, we sometimes enslave
ourselves to certain mindsets.

Conversely, like John Jack, some persons
assume an attitude of being free. Viktor Frankl's

book *Man's Search for Meaning* describes the dynamic and exciting freedom which can be experienced, even in a concentration camp, when a person chooses to love and care for fellow prisoners. I wonder how many black slaves in America were sustained in their physical slavery by choices of attitude.

In America our entire history as a nation for over two centuries could be written from the perspective of the issues of freedom. We claim to be the land of the free and the home of the brave. Our self-perception is that we claimed our freedom as a nation when our ancestors declared our independence from Great Britain in 1776. The Civil War was precipitated over the freedoms claimed by the states, as well as over the issue of slavery. The events of the World Wars, the Korean Conflict, Vietnam, as well as various "police actions" and humanitarian aid operations, all have had to do with freedom.

Struggles with the settlement of the West, with the industrial revolution, with Civil Rights, with court decisions on abortion—all have had to do with freedom. Technological advances—from the washing machine and the automobile to the microwave oven and the Internet—all have had to do with freedom.

But our achievement of "freedom" has been a mixed blessing, according to Will Willimon and Stanley Hauerwas. They are not certain that we have achieved true self-freedom but rather may have achieved only self-centeredness.

We hold these truths to be self-evident, that all men are created equal, that they are endowed by their Creator with certain unalienable rights, that among these are life, liberty, and the pursuit of happiness.

By labeling certain principles [in the *Declaration of Independence*] as naturally "self-evident," by offering equality and rights, the Enlightenment hoped to produce people who were free. Detached from oppressive claims of tradition and community, holding the significance of their lives within themselves as an individual, natural right, being given the independence to fashion their own future, they were to become free.

It was an adventure that held the seeds of its own destruction within itself, within its attenuated definition of human nature and its inadequate vision of human destiny. What we got was not self-freedom but self-centeredness, loneliness, superficiality, and harried consumerism. Free is not how many of our citizens feel—with our overstocked medicine cabinets, burglar alarms, vast ghettos, and drug culture. Eighteen hundred New Yorkers are murdered every year by their fellow citizens in a city whose police department is larger than the standing army of many nations. The adventure went sour.[6]

Whereas the gravestone of John Jack proclaims a slave's attitude of feeling free, we who are "free" often willingly assume the bondage of self-centeredness.

Paul has wisely written in Galatians 5:13: *For you were called to freedom, brothers and sisters, only do not use your freedom as an opportunity for self-indulgence, but through love become slaves to one another.* He might well have foreseen the possibility that we in a "free" nation have, by the choices we have made, become a nation of slaves. What has happened in America today, what Willimon and Hauerwas describe so well, is similar to what had happened in the Roman providence of Galatia during the century after Christ's death.

Paul was expounding on freedom for the early Christians when he wrote his letter to the Galatians, which has been called "The Epistle of Freedom." He writes in Galatians 1:4: *[Jesus] gave Himself for our sins to set us free from the present evil age.* In 5:1: *For freedom, Christ has set us free. Stand firm, therefore, and do not submit again to a yoke of slavery.*

Many of the citizens of Galatia were slave owners. The Apostle used their understanding of the issue of slavery and freedom to remind them of something which was very important, the conflict of Jewish law and freedom. After his Damascus Road experience, he was conscious of the Jewish faith as a religion of laws (man's effort) and the Christian faith as a religion of freedom (God's gift).

After Paul's preaching in Galatia had produced many converts, other Jewish Christians came to Galatia and taught these Gentile converts that they were now subject to the Law in the books of Moses and that to validate their credentials as Christians the Law must be kept, especially law concerning the circumcision of the male converts.

Paul, himself a convert from Judaism, became very angry about this. *"Don't submit to the law,"* he wrote. *"You have been made free in Christ. Salvation is a free gift of God through Jesus Christ."* He reminded them, *"We are not set right with God through rule keeping or good works, but through personal faith in Jesus Christ. God has called you to this free life."* So he advised the Greek converts, *"Don't be circumcised, for circumcision is but a way of submitting to the law."* He was so angry that he said *"If you let these jewizers circumcise you, you might as well let them castrate you."* I would say he was very angry! Don't let anything be your God save God alone! Similarly, the understanding of Christian freedom led Martin Luther to write: "Love God and sin bravely."

While some of the gentile Christians in Galatia had become enslaved to the law, others were becoming enslaved to what Paul calls the *works of the flesh . . . jealousy, anger, strife, quarrels, . . . factions, envy, drunkenness, carousing, and things like that—I am warning you, those who do such things will not inherit the kingdom of God* (Galatians 5:22).

He had already warned the Christians that

> . . . *It is obvious what kind of life develops out of trying to get your own way all the time—loveless, cheap sex, a stinking accumulation of mental and emotional garbage, frenzied and joyless grabs of happiness, trinket gods, magic show religion, paranoic loneliness, cut-throat competition, all consuming yet never satisfied wants, a brutal temper, and impotence to love or be loved, divided homes and divided lives, small-minded and lopsided pursuits, the vicious habit of depersonalizing everyone into a rival, uncontrolled and uncontrollable addictions.*
>
> Galatians 5:19-23 TM

For the people of our time the price of enslavement to "loveless, cheap sex" is well documented. From the fiction of soap operas to the evening news, you do not have to look any farther than your television set to see the bankruptcy of such a life style. The story of Mel Reynolds is such a story. Born poor in rural Mississippi, Reynolds was a scholastic standout at the University of Illinois, studied at Oxford on a Rhodes scholarship and was elected to the U.S. Congress in 1992. Yet in 1995 he went on trial for sexual trysts with teenage girls, was convicted and imprisoned. It is a sad story.

Paul's reference to "all-consuming but never satisfied wants" brings to mind our own culture's love affair with consumerism. Credit cards, often a contemporary blessing, are just as often a terrible enslaving curse. Recently my wife Jane and I traveled half way around the world with only a few dollars and a credit card. Bankers and store clerks in Spain would hand over to me my purchase or a pocketful of pesetas when I would give them my credit card. All I have to do is to pay the bill at the end of the month. And therein lies the curse for many, especially if they are enslaved by Paul's "joyless grabs for happiness" and "trinket gods."

Many people never pay what becomes a revolving credit account, which grows each month until they are prisoners to their own carelessness. This is not good stewardship and it is poor business. We can enslave ourselves to the bondage of materialism and greed.

In May, 1985, Ivan Boesky was the commencement speaker at the School of Business Administration of the University of California at

Berkeley. He astonished most of the western world when he said: "Greed is all right! I think greed is healthy. You can be greedy and still feel good about yourself."

Ivan Boesky's own greed led to his downfall and landed him in prison. His basic claim to fame will be that he was the perpetrator of the biggest insider-trading scandal in the twentieth century. I wonder today if he has had second thoughts about his claim that "greed is all right." Perhaps the saddest part of this story is not just what Boesky said to the graduates but that they greeted it with applause and laughter. These people are now, ten years later, the up-and-coming corporate leaders of America.

Selfishness and greed are but the paving stones of a dead-end street! They are Paul's "frenzied and joyless grab for happiness." In the midst of the greatest and most free country in history, we can choose to lock ourselves in our own jail.

Another enslaving attitude in our country is revealed in statistics on the use of alcohol. Beer consumption among the young is on a dangerously upward trend! "Get all the gusto out of life!" "You only go around once!" These are the messages of colorful, exciting beer commercials which seldom feature anyone older than twenty-five because the target group is much younger and, I might add, more naive and vulnerable. How can we be free if we allow advertisers to control our children's lives?

I don't know where or when we bought into the idea that our freedom naturally gives license for self-gratification but, reading Paul's first century letter, we learn that evidently we are not the first. His message is very clear: we have received the gift of freedom, not for self-gratification, but for the purpose of serving others.

For you are called to freedom, only do not use your freedom as an opportunity for self-indulgence, but through love become slaves to one another (Galatians 5:13).

Helen Keller wrote: "Many persons have a wrong idea of what constitutes true happiness. It is not attained through self-gratification, but through fidelity to a worthy purpose." Albert Schweitzer said: "One thing I know, the only ones among you who will be really happy are those who will seek and find how to serve."

Let us remember that accepting freedom is a part of our Baptismal Vows: "Do you accept the freedom and power God gives you to resist evil, injustice, and oppression in whatever forms they present themselves?"

An acceptance of this freedom means living God's way. Paul tells us how it works:

What happens when we live God's way? He brings gifts into our lives, much the same way that fruit appears in an orchard—things like: affection for others, exuberance about life, serenity. We develop a willingness to stick with things, a sense of compassion in the heart, and a conviction that a basic holiness permeates things and people. We find ourselves involved in loyal commitments, not needing to force our way in life, able to marshal and direct our energies wisely.

Galatians 5:22,23 TM

The slave John Jack set his will to God's will and lived God's way. If you are to become the person you want to be, you must embrace that same freedom.

More than all else, keep watch over your heart,
since here are the wellsprings of life.

Proverbs 4: 23 TJB

"Read" the Right "Books"

Keep your heart with all vigilance, for from it flow the springs of life.

Proverbs 4:23

How does one watch over the heart and keep the heart with all vigilance? Vigilance implies being aware at every moment in life of nurturing one's heart, this most precious part of every personality. That is a tough task, given the easy availability of every kind of printed and imaged material and the popular culture which is producing it. Vigilance requires the understanding that we are feeding our future with every visual image we absorb, every word we read and store in our awesome memory.

With what are you filling your mind? What are the facts and fantasies which you are loading into your conscious and subconscious mind? Do you realize that these become the deeds and actions of tomorrow?

Although we are living in the new age of electronics—characterized by computers, e-mail, fax, tv, cellular phones, and videos—books continue to be sold at rates unparalleled in history, and that includes religious books and Bibles. The continuing popularity of books is true in almost every country in the world. In Russia, book publishing is the second largest industry. (The production and sale of vodka is the largest.) Early fears that the computer screen would completely replace the printed page have thus far proved unfounded. Books have continued to be important in our lives.

In fact, the books a person uses daily are markers for the state of his or her heart. Of the five books I consider to be the most important in your life only one is to be read in the usual fashion.

* * *

Someone told me once that if you want to

write a biography of a person, the first book you need to research is his personal **checkbook**, for there you will learn what was of value to him, what was important in his life. Just take a minute or two and look back over the last three or four months of notations in your checkbook and you will discover what you have valued. O.K., perhaps you'll be looking instead at charge card statements and automatic electronic transfer records, but the idea is the same. The paper trails of some of us would show that we are hopelessly caught up in low-value materialism.

One of the things that is desperately wrong with our lives is that we are identified by how much money we earn and that our need to spend it is almost out of control. Has our national culture, powered by the greatest economic engine ever put together and built on the enormous and unfulfillable needs of the consumer, turned us away from the important affairs of the heart to which Proverbs 4:23 refers? Some persons from other countries seem to think so:

North Americans have to work more in order to buy things. For that reason they spend less time with their families, thinking that to be comfortable is more important for the family than to give them love and time together.

Inez Morales de Rake, Bolivia

In the cities everything travels so fast that we can hardly find people who value cooperation, love, and understanding. They just value their time for money, money, money. The poor dream of having wealth like the rich, and thus there are many robberies and other sorts of crimes.

Leonard Triyono, Indonesia

When people have fewer possessions it is easier for them to be satisfied with what they do have—each other, for instance.

Ellen Orthmann, Netherlands[7]

We are writing checks or using our credit cards or spending our ATM dollars for instant satisfaction. The convenience of these contemporary time-savers has infected our whole value system. We want what we want and we want it now. Most of us have discarded the criteria which served many generations and helped them build solid foundations for their lives: will it last, is it well constructed, does it satisfy a basic and long-term need? Perhaps we need to seriously consider praying

"The Consumer's Prayer":

throwaway bottles
throwaway cans
throwaway friendships
throwaway fans

disposable diapers
disposable plates
disposable people
disposable wastes

instant puddings
instant rice
instant intimacy
instant ice

plastic dishes
plastic laces
plastic flowers
plastic faces

Lord of the living
transcending our lies
infuse us with meaning
recycle our lives[8]

Before World War II, poverty disciplined
many lives. A shortage of money in many house-

holds made us careful about what we spent. Then came the wartime plenty. Decisions were made on the basis of "I want my kids to have it better than I had it!" Now, with more disposable income than ever before, we spend freely and mortgage tomorrow simply because it's there. Is there anyone today who can understand the positive values of poverty?

More than fifty years ago Dorothy Day quoted William James, who looked ahead and saw the rise of this age of insatiable greed and materialism:

> We have grown literally afraid to be poor. We despise anyone who elects to be poor in order to simplify and save his inner life. If he does not join the general scramble, we deem him spiritless and lacking in ambition. We have lost the power even of imagining what the ancient realization of poverty could have meant; the liberation from material attachments, the unbribed soul.[9]

Jesus offered a model for this kind of freedom from materialism: *If someone drags you into court and sues for the shirt off your back, giftwrap your best coat and make a present of it. And if someone takes unfair advantage of you, use the occasion to practice the servant life. No more tit-for-tat stuff. Live generously* (Matthew 5:40 TM).

Remarkable! Radical! Revolutionary! I find myself in a continuous struggle to live in this radical way. I find I need some kind of pattern to follow because I can't always trust my impulses. John Wesley once counseled: Make all you can. Save all you can. Give all you can. I have learned that a good basic formula for money management is to save ten percent, give ten percent, and spend the rest with joy and thanksgiving. In this way I am often able to give more generously than I could have imagined.

"Keeping watch over your heart" requires vigilance over your spending habits. It requires knowing the kind of person you want to become and making sure your spending habits reflect that kind of person.

* * *

Besides the checkbook, another important indicator of the state of the heart is a person's **appointment book** or **calendar**.

Stephen Covey in his book *Seven Habits of Highly Effective People* has given us lessons on the use of time. He helps his readers to an understanding of the various roles we assume (father / mother, boss / employee, friend, church member, director, coach, etc.) and how the balanced life will include *planned* time for each role. For instance, he shows how, even though a man may consider the "professional" or "breadwinning" role to be dominant, that of "father" and that of "husband" are just as vital to the overall development of his effectiveness and must be planned for with the same faithfulness and discipline. He points out that a great deal of pain can come into one's life when success in one role, such as being a successful wage earner or super-professional, has to be balanced against failure in another role, such as parent or spouse.

The written or unwritten daily diary of many of us will reflect that we play out one role with care while every other role is subordinated and crowded into leftover time. The Psalmist writes: *So teach us to number our days that we may apply our hearts unto wisdom* (Psalms 90:12 KJV). If we are wise, we will "apply our hearts" to balancing our lives so that we have time for the most important things.

* * *

A third book which will serve as the indicator of the state of the heart is a person's **journal**. While my appointment book records where I go, what I do, and with whom, my journal reflects why I am doing what I'm doing and what I am thinking—sometimes fantasizing—about. My journal records my efforts to get to know God, to relate to the significant persons in my life, and to deal with events as they occur.

A journal, more than anything else, will record who I am spiritually. If I am truly, scathingly honest with myself when I write in my journal, I will reveal myself in ways that I do in no way other than in my prayers of confession to God. When I read it, it will reveal my self to me.

I encourage you to consider keeping a journal. As you struggle to keep your heart with all vigilance, it is important for your journal to record those ideas and feelings which reside in your heart. Be honest with your journal, and you will be able to track the hidden thoughts and overt actions which may be keeping you from becoming the person you want to be.

* * *

Another book that becomes an aid in keeping watch over your heart is your **hymnal**.

The hymns and gospel songs I have sung since I was a boy have become a part of my life that will never leave me. Even in rural Alabama, far from the great cathedrals with their beautiful pipe organs and handsomely robed choirs, we sang great and powerful hymns. Many were the compositions of Charles Wesley, who was present at the birth of Methodism and who penned hundreds of inspiring songs, most of which are as meaningful today as in the eighteenth century:

> O for a thousand tongues to sing
> my great Redeemer's praise,
> the glories of my God and King,
> the triumphs of his grace.
>
> Jesus! The name that charms our fears,
> that bids our sorrows cease;
> 'tis music in the sinner's ears,
> 'tis life, and health, and peace!
> Charles Wesley, 1739

One day while I was recuperating from an

injury I was at home alone, sitting in a comfortable chair in the living room. I was deeply aware of both the pain in my leg and the hovering depression that seemed to increase with each additional week of a long recovery. The house was quiet. The sun, slanting through the trees outside, came in the window to make a bright square on the carpet just a few feet from me. The quiet deepened. With the sun, into my mind came, unbidden, an Afro-American spiritual I had learned long ago as a child at church in Marengo County:

> There is a balm in Gilead
> to make the wounded whole;
> There is a balm in Gilead
> to heal the sinsick soul.
>
> Sometimes I feel discouraged,
> and think my work's in vain.
> But then the Holy Spirit
> revives my soul again.

Those kinds of recollections have blessed my life and work again and again.

One day my pastoral visits took me to a

nursing home where I was to call on a woman in the advanced stages of Alzheimer's Disease. She had rarely recognized me on previous visits. As I walked quietly into the room I heard a faint melody coming from the fragile body on the bed. She was lying with her eyes closed, tremulously singing a hymn.

> My Jesus, I love thee,
> I know thou art mine . . . .
> My gracious Redeemer,
> my Savior art thou,
> If ever I loved thee,
> my Jesus, 'tis now.
> William R. Featherstone, 1864

Those words and the melody had been fixed in her mind during an active and faithful Christian life, and now God was helping her use them to move on through a tough stage in her life. I stood for another moment, singing quietly with her, and then went about my other visits, marveling that the words and music of her hymnbook continue to minister to her when a seminary full of ministers couldn't have reached her.

How will you start to become the person you want to be? You could start by singing with the congregation on Sunday morning, thus sharing your faith and storing those words in your heart.

* * *

With your checkbook, your appointment book, and your private journal to measure the true quality of your life, with your hymnal to offer sustenance, there is another book that will provide the guidance and reassurance you will need to make the changes necessary for becoming the person you want to be. It is the **Bible**.

The Bible is important to this process for many reasons. For example, it tells the stories of the lives of our faith ancestors. There was Abraham, whose faith in God was so strong he would have sacrificed his own son even as God was to do. There was Abraham's son Isaac, who prospered under God's direction, and Isaac's son Jacob, whose rivalry with his brother separated the family, and Jacob's son Joseph, who forgave the brothers who wronged him. To these men God renewed the covenant he had made with Abraham. And there was Moses, who led

God's chosen people out of Egyptian bondage. There was the fearless but very human prophet Elijah, and there was David the shepherd king, who eloquently sang God's praise in the Psalms.

And, of course, Jesus. Always Jesus. The New Testament story of Jesus teaches us how to live and shows us very clearly how to be disciples.

> Pray for one another.
> Go the second mile.
> Turn the other cheek.
> Be peacemakers.
> Hunger and thirst for righteousness.
> Ask and receive, seek and find.
> Knock and move through the open door.
> Be the light of the world,
> the salt of the earth.
> Witness to the grace and goodness of
> God.

The story of Jesus is a deep mine, full of the precious gems of his teachings.

* * *

The Bible also tells us that God is involved in our lives and that we are never alone. The Holy Spirit will come to us, God present with us. These words are not just ancient history; they are contemporary comfort.

The Bible tells us that we will be judged by the actions of our lives. The Bible also teaches that there is forgiveness, that God's grace reconciles us unto himself and gives to us the ministry of reconciliation. There is grace, hope, and love available for us.

Basically, [the Bible] is a love story between God and humanity; it is a story of a covenant made, broken, and renewed, again and again. God as creator, redeemer, and perfecter loves each creature, personally and as members of the whole human community. In return, we are expected to love God, ourselves, and each other.

The Bible is a book of faith; that is, the Bible presents a way to perceive life in general and our lives in particular. The Bible is a book of revelation; that is, the Bible unveils those intimate relationships with God experienced by others so that we might share in them. The Bible is a book of vocation; that is, the Bible gives us a vision of how we ought to live our lives with God and each other day by day.

We need to enlarge our grasp of this love story—to learn it more completely, to understand it more deeply, to possess it more personally, and to live it more fully. This is a lifelong task.[10]

There is no way to overstate the power that the Bible can have in your life. If you make its story your story, you will begin to change, and life around you will begin to change.

Of all the books you have read or will read, this one will provide the wellsprings to enable you to become the person you yearn to be.

What happens to a dream
deferred?
Does it dry up
like a raisin in the sun?
Or fester like a sore—
And then run?
Does it stink like rotten meat?
Or crust and sugar over—
like a syrupy sweet?

Maybe it just sags
like a heavy load.

Or does it explode?

"Harlem"
Langston Hughes 1902-1967

Live Your Dream

What is becoming of your dream? If—as Langston Hughes' poem suggests—it is just lying there, drying out or festering up or crusting over or sagging into a heavy load, then it is time to do something about it!

Oswald Chambers says flatly that "Dreaming about a thing in order to do it properly is right; but dreaming about it when we should be doing it is wrong."[11]

Having a dream is easy. It is accomplishing the dream, living it, maintaining it that is difficult.

When we are quite young, just becoming aware of boys—or girls, as the case may be—the dreams we dream are mostly romantic fantasies. A little older, we fantasize about how we will be in the future. Few of these kinds of dreams are ever lived—and perhaps it is just as well!

Patricia Wilson recites youthful fantasies in her book *How Can I Be Over the Hill.*

> When I am older, I will live a mad, bohemian lifestyle life on the Continent. I will be perpetually tanned and ravishing, keeping company with a small, exclusive, talented circle of friends. My husband will murmur to me in French as we glide along in our Rolls-Royce. My children will be named Sarah and Jonothan the Vth and will be taken care of by Miss Billingston, not me.[12]

Our own dreams for the future may have been—may still be!—just as fanciful. Or perhaps they have changed to more identifiable goals.

To be thin.

To be beautiful or handsome.

To be Mother of the Year or Coach of the All Stars or the boss at work.

To live in a beautiful, spotless house.

To have the kind of job that calls for a designer briefcase and an up-to-date passport.

To marry the perfect mate.

The dream marriage event occurs almost every weekend in the sanctuary of the church where I serve. These weddings are lovely and exciting. All brides are beautiful and all grooms are excited. Getting married is a relatively easy dream to attain because it is stimulating and invigorating. The challenge is to hold the marriage together when love is tired, when trust is betrayed, when compassion just cannot be found. The challenge is to live the dream.

Many couples I know have given up right at the time they might be getting to know each other. Some have given up even sooner! Too many were seduced by dreams of romance without making a commitment to hard work.

I recently attended a party celebrating a couple's fiftieth wedding anniversary. Fifty years! There are a lot of those in the church family. It is not so unusual among church members, but it is unusual in the world beyond the church. As a matter of fact, in Escambia County in a recent year, 3,118 couples were married. Divorces counted in the same year numbered 1,723, over half the number of marriages. It is easy to have a dream. It is more difficult to keep the dream alive.

The members of my graduating class at Emory University's Candler School of Theology in 1968 left school with such excitement and visions of glory! About a third of them are today not in this profession. I had a great uncle who was for twenty years pastor of University Baptist Church in Tuscaloosa, Alabama. Uncle Horace jokingly said to me one day, "The clergy is a great profession. You only have to work on Sunday. The only problem is that Sunday comes every day." And I have found his statement to be accurate, as did, no doubt, everyone else in my graduating class. Living the dream requires daily effort.

In Clifford Irving's novel *Final Argument*, Ted Jaffe, a wealthy attorney, muses:

> I remembered how once I had wanted to be of service, how my deepest ambition had been to argue a case before the Supreme Court and save an innocent man's life. In the quest for creature comfort and security, somehow that had faded from my consciousness. Just a short while ago I'd thought that I had almost everything I wanted. All that blocked my path

to the happiest of endings, I'd decided, was the economic recession and the torment of my son.

How shallow I had become in these years. Do we do the right thing, I wondered, by giving up our youthful fantasies? [13]

On August 28, 1963, Martin Luther King, Jr., stirred the heart of the nation with his speech to a huge audience on the mall in Washington, D.C. "I have a dream," he said, "that one day we will judge the worth of a man by the character of his soul, not the color of his skin." Twenty-five years after that stirring occasion I attended a parade in Dr. King's honor in Pensacola. It was a national holiday and the theme was "Living the Dream." While King's dream is far from realized, attitudes about race have continued to improve in the last quarter-century. I thank God that many, many people of all colors are working today to keep this visionary's dream alive.

I noticed on an office desk recently one of those little stand-up signs that had the letters TCB on it. When I asked the meaning, I was told it stands for *Taking Care of Business*. Jesus said "Seek first the Kingdom of God," or maybe he said "TCB."

Take care of business if you want to realize your dream and live it. Put first things first!

Jesus illustrated the importance of persistence in the story of the woman who came to borrow some bread from a neighbor late at night. She knocked on his door until he finally got up. He came to the door, not because he wanted to help out his neighbor but because she would not quit knocking and calling his name until he opened the door. Don't give up!

It is important to surround yourself with persons who share your dream, not with those who don't believe in dreams. Paul wrote *Do not pair yourself with unbelievers.* Your associates, your friends, your family have a great influence on you. So do the persons who have dreamed and lived their dreams before you.

This concept has been beautifully illustrated in the musical *Seaplane*, written to celebrate the first air crossing of the Atlantic. Carolyn and Jack Fleming's lyrics, set to music by Allen Pote, apply to all of life. We seldom succeed at a dreamed-of venture without the help of others.

To build a dream
      takes more
            than one of us
And even then
  we may never see just when
Or where the dream will end.

Inspiration comes from knowing those
Who have gone before,
Who have said,
      "Take a chance!"
          "Be of courage!"
               "Open up the door!"
We may never see just when or where
      the road will end.
Strong determination comes
      from those who have gone before,
Who have worked and struggled,
      never giving up,
          knowing there is more.
We may never know
      just how far a dream will go.
We can only hope to make it grow.
We can stand on the shoulders
      of dreamers before us,
          hearing their echoes,
          joining the chorus.
Together, we can build a dream!

The calling of God for Christians today is to live the dream. Don't lose it. Christian people can model for the larger world the fact that dreams can be lived and realized. Nothing is set, permanent, determined. Love can be found. Integrity is achievable. Peace can rule in our world. Happiness can be experienced. Our personal hopes can shape our tomorrows. Dreams can be lived! You can become the person you want to be!

A Grace for Dieters

Are there graces for lettuce, Lord?

And low-fat, meat-free, fun-free meals?

I need you to send me words for blessing this paltry meal before me, Lord, for it is difficult to feel grateful for these skimpy portions when all I think of are the foods not on my plate.

Help me change that thought, to make peace with choosing not to eat them, for I need help in becoming the healthier person I want to be.

Hold up for me a mirror of the new creation you see me to be, for I need a companion at this table, Lord.[14]

Margaret Anne Huffman

Develop an Attitude of Gratitude

When upon life's billows you are tempest tossed;
When you are discouraged thinking all is lost;
Count your many blessings, name them one by one,
And it will surprise you what the Lord has done.

Johnson Oatman, Jr., 1897

Back in Marengo County we used to sing this song, called "Count Your Blessings." Some folks forget to count their blessings. They are worn out from counting and recounting the bad things that have happened to them in the past. They are worried about what may happen tomorrow. And they are already in the middle of an uncertain today. But if they would just stop for a moment and count their blessings, they would be surprised what the Lord has done. And if they would be thankful in their quiet times for those things, actually naming those good things, then they would be on the road to becoming the positive, life-affirming persons they long to be.

While I remember vividly the thankfulness on taking that momentous first step on my own feet after two years in a wheel chair and on crutches, I am surprised that I remember just as vividly the overwhelming sense of relief and gratitude which came from the brief moments of peace and rest following times of great pain. Such moments come to those who are conditioned by grateful hearts.

One year when the major league Baseball Hall of Fame held its induction ceremony, a sportscaster asked Rod Carew, one of the inductees, to describe the difference between the old-timers and the players of today. Carew didn't say anything about physical difference or athletic skills. He simply said, "The old-timers were much more appreciative."

Gratitude can be God's change agent for our

lives. In the presence of genuine gratitude bad digestion may improve. Footsteps can develop a spring. Relationships can change. Even the look in people's eyes can be different.

Now, I know that it is not possible to change the genetic makeup which causes us to be who we are. Also, neither you nor I can change our early childhood environments. Even God does not offer to change those things. Often it is not possible to change the environment in which we currently live and work. But God can help us change the way we think about the past and about ourselves and about those around us. Our minds, our attitudes, can be transformed. We can change from perpetual, festering ingratitude to genuine, life-changing gratitude.

One of the many transforming events in Jesus' ministry occurred on the day he healed ten persons who had leprosy.

On the way to Jerusalem Jesus was going through the region between Samaria and Galilee. As he entered a village, ten lepers approached him. Keeping their distance, they called out, saying, "Jesus, Master, have mercy on us!" When he saw them, he said to them, "Go and show yourselves to the priests." And as they went, they were made clean. Then one of them, when he saw that he was healed, turned back, praising God with a loud voice. He prostrated himself at Jesus' feet and thanked him. And he was a Samaritan. Then Jesus asked, "Were not ten made clean? But the other nine, where are they? Was none of them found to return and give praise to God except this foreigner?" Then he said to him, "Get up and go on your way; your faith has made you well."   Luke 17:12

Leprosy was then a debilitating, contagious disease which often claimed the feet and hands of its victims and left them limping along, begging for food. The lepers lived in shacks outside the villages where their families resided, along with other persons who had been declared unclean and who had been forced to leave their families. Jesus heard them call out from their need and healed them. Then he told them to go to Jerusalem and offer themselves at their place of worship. Jesus was obviously pleased that one of them returned to say "thank you." He sent that healed leper on his way with a blessing.

I have found that receiving blessings is almost

always the result of exhibiting a spirit of thankfulness.

The leper asked. He was obedient. He said "Thank you."

Asking.

Being Obedient.

Saying "Thank You."

These are the keys which unlock the door to faith's gifts. A thankful heart sees life through the eyes of gratitude. It sees what one has, not what one does not have. It sees clearly that all of life is gift. It enables us to understand, like the Apostle Paul, that . . . *all things work together for good for those who love God, who are called according to his purpose* (Romans 8:28).

I cannot see clearly through my left eye. I always see a smudge or a blur, as if someone needs to turn the knob in the projection booth. So what I have had to do is get used to looking out of my right eye, through which I see clearly. To see life out of the right eye with the desired clarity of vision is to look at life with a thankful heart. The tenth leper saw life out of his right eye, for he saw clearly that life is a blessing and that Jesus is the change agent.

In a sense, persons who regularly meet together in worship are like the tenth leper, who returned to Jesus to say "thank you." In many ways we have been diseased or injured. We cry out for healing and find it in Jesus. We return to worship to say "thank you."

There are so many reasons to be thankful! If you do not habitually find reasons to thank God, I can think of several for you. First, thank God that you are alive!

One of the hymns of Charles Wesley expresses thankfulness for the safe return to worship of the members of his congregation:

> And are we yet alive,
> and see each other's face?
> Glory and thanks to Jesus give
> for his almighty grace.
>
> What troubles have we seen,
> what mighty conflicts past,
> fighting without, and fears within,
> since we assembled last?

Yet out of all, the Lord
hath brought us by his love
and still he doth his help afford
and hides our life above.
Charles Wesley, 1749

We have troubles, fightings without and fears within. But our God is like a mighty fortress, like a nurturing mother, like a refuge and strength, like a shepherd, like a forgiving father welcoming the prodigal son home, like a great physician. For this we must be thankful. *Let us come into his presence with thanksgiving* . . . (Psalms 95:2).

Shortly after two recent hurricanes on the Gulf Coast I met in Minneapolis a man from the western United States who was quite interested in what had happened in the Pensacola area, where I live. In the course of our conversation he said to me, "Why do you continue to live in a place where there is such danger?"

I asked him, "Now, where did you say you were from?"

To which he responded with the name of a town located squarely on the earthquake fault line just out of Los Angeles!

I kindly chose not to remind him of the dangers where he lived. Wherever you live, there are dangers. This truth came home to me when my family headed north in the evacuation prompted by Hurricane Opal. The storm followed us all the way! A few days later, returning home in heavy south-bound traffic, we saw a truck towing a car which had obviously been squashed by a fallen tree. In the back window was a homemade sign: "You can run but you can't hide!"

The fact is that if we are alive, vitally alive, in our faith, even the threat of danger and death does not debilitate us.

An unexpected insight into gratitude comes from Arthur Gordon's book *A Touch of Wonder*:

> I remember a cold December afternoon years ago when I was in my early twenties. A friend and I were winding up a day of duck hunting. We were picking up the decoys when a flight of Canada geese came by. They drove right across the sunset, so low that you could see their wing tips reflected in the burnished water. The sight was so magnificent that I

exclaimed, "Look at that! Makes you grateful just to be alive!"

And my friend said quietly, "Grateful to whom?"

That was all he said, but his words reminded me of this: "how can one be grateful for a gift without acknowledging a Giver?" It is not always easy to see life through the experience of gratitude, but when I do, all of life becomes precious.[15]

From people to whom all things in life were gifts comes this Shaker hymn:

'Tis the gift to be simple,
'Tis the gift to be free,
'Tis the gift to come down
Where we ought to be.

It reminds us that we should express gratitude for all things.

Remember Forrest Gump? The movie is a delightful, entertaining story of a successful Southerner with an IQ slightly below normal. Forrest has been raised by his mother, who lavished love on him and succeeded in filling his head with spiritual wisdom. Although he is slow and naive, somehow fortune always smiles on him. He comes through situations which appear destined to destroy his self-esteem, his joy of life, and any chance at success. He seems incapable of failure as an athlete in college, as a soldier in Vietnam, and as a shrimp boat operator. The key to his unusual success is that he sees life differently from others even though they are smarter and quicker than he is.

One of his favorite sayings, repeated several times throughout the movie, is "Mama always did say, 'Life is like a box of chocolates. You never know what you're gonna get.'"

Whatever we get, there is much to be grateful for. We are quick to ask for things. We are some-what slower to be obedient to the way we are directed. And we are slower still to say "thank you."

Do you remember to say "thank you" to God? Have you said "thank you" for a good night's sleep? An autumn day of blue sky and sunshine? The unexpected voice of a distant friend on the tele-phone? A car battery that works? Uncontrollable laughter, unashamed tears, aspirin, your life mate, your children, your grandchildren? You make your own list. Mine includes a body that, in spite of its batterings, is more complex and works better than all the electronic circuitry in existence.

On my list, too, are children who skip down the aisle at worship services, people over forty who look over forty, teenagers who remind us to laugh at ourselves, electric light bulbs, comfortable shoes and indoor restrooms.

Margaret Anne Huffman's prayer for dieters, quoted at the beginning of this chapter, illustrates the struggles to be grateful for low-fat meals with skinny portions. She asks for a mirror that will show her the new creation she will be. It is important to keep that longed-for image in front of us, whether we are struggling for new well-being or a new being.

Gratitude and thanksgiving, even for the diet meal that you don't particularly like, are a vital part of becoming your best self.

You can become the person you want to be by keeping awareness and thankfulness alive in your heart, by approaching every day when you awaken with the words, *This is the day that the Lord has made; Let us rejoice and be glad in it* (Psalms 118:24).

You can change the look on your face by being aware and thankful. You can change your relationships by being aware and thankful. You can change the course of your life by being aware and thankful.

Remember how the tenth leper became a new person and received a blessing.

Ask.

Be Obedient.

Be Thankful.

Nobody truly occupies a station in life anymore. There are displaced persons everywhere.

Saul Bellow

Remember Who You Are

"Mom, I don't have nothing to live up to."

As sung by Bob Dylan

What a sad voice is crying out in Bob Dylan's lyrics! Fortunately, most of us have something to live up to, a family and faith heritage that is better than society's compromised and tarnished expectations.

When we were teenagers, my dad started saying to my older brother and me as we would leave the house at night, "Now, boys, remember who you are." He was saying that he didn't want us to get in trouble, didn't want us to hurt ourselves and didn't want us to embarrass him or Mom. He was probably saying even a lot more than that, but we understood,

117

and his brief admonition probably kept us out of jail and certainly out of a lot of mischief!

"Remember who you are." Over the years I have often said that to persons I cared about. "Remember who you are." In other words, don't compromise your beliefs, your self-understanding, your integrity, your reputation.

A news reporter once said to Franklin Delano Roosevelt, then president of the United States, "Your son Quentin is certainly conducting himself in a way that would make any father proud."

And the President said, "Well, he had better. He is a Roosevelt, you know." Holding on to family tradition is important.

Individuals who have no worthy family tradition, or who ignore their family tradition, get in trouble with themselves and with their families and with the law. One of the serious problems in contemporary society is that there is such confusion in the minds of the young, planted there either by their own crazy, unprincipled families or by the absurd moral practices constantly portrayed on television and in movies.

Bob Dylan sings, "Mom, I don't have nothing to live up to." I wonder if that is not because Dylan had intentionally cut himself off from the past and had made no effort to understand his heritage. It takes, as Edward Sellner writes,

> . . . some digging in the ruins, some re-collecting of our pasts. We only learn from the past when we are knowledgeable and appreciative of it. Recalling our histories, both familial and ecclesial, is a way of celebrating our inheritance, claiming it as ours, and most important, adding to it. This celebration includes both prayer and storytelling . . . the remembrance of saving deeds that put us in touch with the living presence of God and our continuity with the past.
>
> One of the most powerful forms of prayer is that of remembering and identifying all those who have mentored us in a significant way. [16]

The Apostle Paul wrote to the young church in Thessalonica: *Stand firm and hold fast to the traditions that you were taught by us* (Second Thessalonians 2:15).

He was saying "Remember who you are."

The letters to that church were the earliest of those written by the Apostle. Apparently the church had become confused as to his teachings concerning what was referred to as "the coming day of the Lord" or "the second coming of Jesus." The people had assumed that the last days had begun and so they had stopped working and were doing little more than lying around waiting. Paul writes to them and tells them, get a job, get busy, and while you are busy, "hold fast to the tradition which has been passed to you."

The church where I am privileged to serve was founded more than one hundred seventy-five years ago. It has taught one generation after another a grand tradition of beliefs and moral behavior. Unlike the son, whose voice Bob Dylan uses when he sings, "Mom, I don't have nothing to live up to," the children of the church have the traditions of the faith to hold to. We must teach them how to remember who they are.

Who we are is bound up in our basic beliefs. These beliefs we get within the family, certainly, but they are specifically articulated and expounded within the church.

We believe in God, who is the Creating Father, the Redeeming Son, and the Ever-present Spirit—one sovereign and all-powerful God, but One who is known in his creation, in his acts of redemption and in the ongoing work of God the Holy Spirit. We believe that what we believe about God shapes how we treat others.

We strive to live our lives according to the teachings of Jesus Christ, as he instructed *Do unto others as you would have them do unto you*. In a larger sense we strive not to do anything which is in conflict with the teachings and the spirit of Jesus. St. Paul's faith was Christ-centered. He wrote in Colossians 1:17: . . . *in him all things hold together.*

What we believe defines who we are and affects how we handle successes and setbacks. In Paul's later letters, the ones written from jail in Rome (Ephesians, Philippians, Colossians, and Philemon), he affirms a confident faith forged in the crucible of personal suffering. Those letters have taught me that in grim surroundings, in the midst of suffering, God will see us through any calamity. No matter what adverse situation we may face—personal attack, physical affliction, hardship or disaster—the strength and ability to get through it all comes from God, through our confidence in the beliefs we have forged, beliefs that are at the core of who we are. When I see a couple, especially a couple with children, who are considering divorce, I want to say to them "You don't have to run. Stay and work it out. Rely on your beliefs. There is hope."

A poem Dietrich Bonhoeffer wrote in a Nazi prison illustrates the continual battle inside our minds and hearts as we struggle through the really tough places in our lives to maintain our integrity, to know who we are.

Who am I? They often tell me
I would step from my cell's confinement
calmly, cheerfully, firmly,
like a squire from his country house.

Who am I? They often tell me
I would talk to my warders
freely and friendly and clearly,
as though it were mine to command.

Who am I? They also tell me
I would bear the days of misfortune
equably, smilingly, proudly,
like one accustomed to win.

Am I really all that which other men tell of?
Or am I only what I know of myself?
restless and longing and sick, like a bird in a cage,
struggling for breath, as though hands were
          compressing my throat,
yearning for colours, flowers, for voices of birds,
thirsting for words of kindness, for neighborliness,
trembling with anger at despotisms and petty
          humiliation,
tossing in expectation of great events,
powerless trembling for friends at an infinite
          distance,
weary and empty at praying, at thinking, at
          making,
faint, and ready to say farewell to it all?

Who am I? This or the other?
Am I one person today, and tomorrow another?
Am I both at once?   A hypocrite before others,
and before myself a contemptibly woebegone
          weakling?
Or is something within me still like a beaten army,
fleeing in disorder from victory already achieved?

Who am I? They mock, these lonely questions of
    mine.
Whoever I am, thou knowest, O God,
    I am thine!

In his experience in prison, Paul learned to be
content, regardless of his circumstances: *I know what
it is to have little, and I know what it is to have plenty.
In any and all circumstances I have learned the secret of
being well-fed and of going hungry, of having plenty and
of being in need* (Philippians 4:12).

What we believe draws us to Christian fellowship. It does not instruct us to become foot-loose
and fancy-free individuals, to simply do what feels
good. Our tradition tells us that it is right to have a
burden for the larger community. Our individual
rights and privileges are to be second to the common
good. We learn in our tradition that the pursuit of
individual happiness is not the pathway for
fulfillment. Unrestricted liberty is not the goal for
God's people. Our Christian tradition has taught us
that it may appear as if the best way to have life,
freedom, and happiness is to avoid the world's
brokenness, sickness, and suffering; but the truth is

just the opposite.

We have a grand and wonderful heritage! There have been passed on to us, and we are trying to pass on to others, our moral and faith systems, which help us to live with dignity and die with confidence.

"How do I become the person I want to be?"

Remember who you are.

Jesus opened himself to the seren-
dipitous future, to the random, to the
surprising, to the strange. Like every Jewish
prophet before him, Jesus could both see
where he was going and yet be surprised by
how God got him there and by what he
found when he got there. Jesus taught that
only when we give ourselves away, and open
our outlooks and obsessions to the mysteries
of the Spirit, can we be truly alive.[17]

Leonard Sweet

Trust the Power and
Keep Your
Foot Off the Hose

In the hurricanes which attack the Gulf coast we see nature's furious power and destructive energy. It is awesome and sometimes frightening. Wind, wrenching trees out of the ground. Tons of sand and water, surging forward to move buildings off their foundations and strip away huge, lovely dunes. Meteorologists try to explain the recent unusual years for storms and point to certain atmospheric conditions which encouraged the increase in this phenomenon. They mention an extremely wet spring and summer season in West Africa, the ozone hole over Antarctica, and the change in the high level wind over the Pacific called "El Nino."

Perhaps they are merely attempting to explain the unexplainable, but their explanations make a lot more sense than the radio preacher who said that God's judgment has come down on the "sinful" ones who live along the Gulf Coast. Nature has claimed our attention—but God's judgment? Please! Such an explanation insults God's goodness and our intelligence. What we know beyond a shadow of a doubt is that nature has a powerful, mysterious side as well as a predictable one.

We know, as well, that there is a mysterious power and strength available to God's people, which is equally remarkable and as amazing and unexplainable as Nature's Power. Jesus spoke of this power when he said that faith, even the amount in a tiny seed, can move mountains: *The simple truth is that if you had a mere kernel of faith, a poppy seed, say, you would tell this mountain, 'Move!' and it would move. There is nothing you wouldn't be able to tackle* (Matthew 17:20,21 TM).

Jesus spoke of this power a number of times. And every time this power is mentioned in the New

Testament it is with the recognition that it comes as a remarkably strange and mysterious force. As Leonard Sweet has noted, "Jesus embraced the unknown, risked living on 'the edge of chaos,' and in taking risks he opened windows to the wonders of eternity."[18]

Trusting the power is really opening yourself to the unknown, yet there is a huge need for power in our lives. We need power to understand, to forgive, to overcome, to accept, and to change. We want and need power to overcome obstacles: the trauma of a broken leg or a broken heart, the despair of a lost relationship or a lost job.

Jesus spoke of the way to the source of power: *"If you abide in me, and my words abide in you, ask for whatever you wish, and it will be done for you"* (John 15:7).

Karen Evans is Director of Education and Children's Ministries in the church where I am pastor. I remember a children's sermon which she preached. She had brought a small table lamp which she placed near the altar rail, where the children could see it. As she spoke to the kids, she kept trying to turn it on, and her frustration was obvious to them and to the whole congregation. Finally two or three of the children blurted out, as she knew they would, "Miss Karen, it's not plugged in!" Her point was made. If you abide in Christ, if you stay connected, if you are plugged in, you can get the power! That was the lesson.

Another promise Jesus made is very similar: *So I tell you, whatever you ask for in prayer, believe that you have received it, and it will be yours* (Mark 11:24).

Before he left them, Jesus spoke to his disciples of special power for ministry and living: *"But you will receive power when the Holy Spirit has come upon you; and you will be my witnesses in Jerusalem, in all Judea and Samaria, and to the ends of the earth"* (Acts 1:8).

The disciples needed that kind of dynamic power after Jesus left, a power that took the form of sheer physical energy and endurance—the power to endure Roman imprisonment and banishment, to recuperate from beatings and illness and shipwreck and starvation.[19]

The promise of power was extended by the

apostle Paul, the apologist of the early church: *I can do all things through him who strengthens me* (Philippians 4:13).

Paul leaves no doubt as to the source of empowerment: *Now to him who by the power at work within us is able to accomplish abundantly far more than all we can ask or imagine, to him be glory in the church and in Christ Jesus to all generations, for ever and ever. Amen* (Ephesians 3:20).

I value Eugene Peterson's translation of this verse: *God can do anything, you know—far more than you could ever imagine or guess or request in your wildest dreams! He does it not by pushing us around but by working within us, his Spirit deeply and gently within us* (Ephesians 3:20,21 TM).

You may have your doubts that this power to overcome, this strength to endure, is available to you and me. Did Jesus really mean, *"Whatever you ask for in prayer, believe that you have received it, and it will be yours"*? Is it true that *"all things are possible to him who believes"*?

It is God's word! You can argue against what it says all day long, and I can stand with you on your side and come up with as many qualifications and limitations to these statements from scripture as you can! But the word is still there. It still stands: *Whatever you ask for in prayer, believe that you have received it, and it will be yours.*

Now suppose it is possible. Suppose that it can be done. Then what? Although we cannot *control* God nor can we control how and when he gives his gifts, such as this power, we *can* create an environment in which his gift of power is most likely to be experienced. Just as the atmosphere of the earth is conducive to creating unusual hurricanes, so also we can create an atmosphere which encourages the power of God to be evidenced in our lives.

For two thousand years Christians have devised "holy habits" as the means of creating the atmosphere or environment in which the gift of God's power to individuals is encouraged. The habits have hardly changed over the centuries, and the discipline of regular practice is just as valuable today as ever. Cultivating holy habits will enable you to be more receptive to God's power. What are "holy habits?"

❧Praying regularly and cultivating a positive, believing spirit. Do you have a planned time for this kind of activity?

❧Performing acts of kindness and generosity. Do you ever perform random acts of kindness and senseless acts of love?

❧Participating in group worship and singing the hymns of the faith. Do you make attendance at worship a priority?

❧Choosing a healthy lifestyle. Do you eat a balanced diet, get the right kind of exercise, and genuine, peaceful rest?

❧Being obedient to the high moral standards of the Bible and the community. Do you use the Bible to discern what high standards really are?

❧Adopting a simpler, quieter life style. Do you make any attempt to rid your life of unnecessary trappings?

When I was a boy I used to go hunting with my father. We hunted in an age and place where there were few fences. It was easy to get lost, so my Dad taught me how to read a compass. He would occasionally become frustrated when I didn't hold the compass perfectly still while taking a reading. I can hear him, almost half a century later, when he would speak loudly and emphatically to me, "Be still, if you want to read the compass."

Our holy habits are the points on the compass. If we remain steady as we follow the needle's direction, we won't lose our way. The Psalmist wrote: *"Be still and know that I am God"* (Psalms 46:10). Be still, if you want to read the compass.

There is a story told by a grandfather about his little grandson who inadvertently stood on the hose when his grandfather was watering the lawn.

"Why did you make the water stop, Granddaddy?"

I had to explain to him that his foot pressure held back the water, but that once he got off the hose the water would flow quite naturally.

This is a good lesson in living, for how often do we, every day of our lives, put our foot on the hose and prevent Divine Power from helping us with our problems? If you find life hard and difficult; if you cannot get along with people; if you show no progress in your daily work; then look within yourself, for you have somehow got your foot on the hose.[20]

The pressure blocking the power flow may come from some hidden sin or secret immorality. It is more likely to come from our failure to maintain our "holy habits." Of one thing I am sure. Maintaining the connection, staying plugged in, unblocking the power flow, is necessary if you are to become the person you want to be.

What we call the beginning
is often the end
And to make an end
is to make a beginning.
The end is where we start from.

T. S. Eliot
Four Quartets,
Little Gidding

The End—
or the Beginning?

"Is it the end or the beginning?" she asked me.

I was visiting that day in the nursing home. I knew she was dying. She knew she was dying. Yet she sat a little straighter in her wheelchair as we visited. Her eyes were more questioning than frightened. She talked of the taste of a tall glass of iced tea, the blandness of nursing home food. We talked of many things—the church, her family. She wondered about the fact that she seemed to be living long after her obviously useful days were over. We wondered if the future would bring as many changes as the past.

Her eyes changed when her granddaughter

came into the room. The granddaughter, tender and caring, greeted us, then gently laid her four-month-old baby in her great-grandmother's arms.

And that was when I saw it! The gleam of joy in her eyes. Just for a fleeting moment the answer was evident to the question she posed: "Is it the end or the beginning of life? Is it the end for me and the beginning for her? Is it a new beginning for us both? What do you think, preacher?" she asked with her eyes. "You're supposed to know about such things. What do you think about this?"

In *Who is Man?* Abraham Heschel writes, "The authentic individual is neither an end nor a beginning but a link between ages, both memory and expectation."

One thing for sure, it is not always easy to determine whether human events are endings or beginnings. We may lament the end of childhood but does not adolescence mark the beginning of maturity? Cannot a day in divorce court ending a marriage be the beginning of a new life for some? Does not the end of one's professional life often mark the beginning of an exciting new personal career? Is death the end of life or the beginning of eternal life?

Certainly, no one could ever say that Jesus' death was the end of his life. He is more alive today than ever before. Even in the former Soviet Union, where for seventy years Russians suffered for believing in Jesus Christ, Jesus is a living reality to millions.

As we approach the year 2000 and the new millennium, we begin to hear a lot of talk about the end of the age. It is not unusual that, as we move toward the end of the century, people begin to think and talk about the end times. It happens every hundred years, I guess. But the end of the millennium? Wow!

Every spring when I was growing up in Marengo County one of the teachers in our high school would invite the junior and senior classes to come to her church on a Wednesday night for her pastor's Annual End-of-the-World Sermon. If I sit real still and quiet and let my mind take me back thirty-odd years, I can yet smell the fumes of hell's flames and hear the weeping and gnashing of teeth, described by the impassioned pastor. The end was near and we needed to prepare, said he in his Annual End-of-the-World Sermon.

It was probably a very smart thing to carry the students to that little country church. Most of the boys never had a thought about anything beyond hunting, sports, or sex—not necessarily in that order. I'm not sure what the girls thought about, although at least one of those same items was probably in their awareness. We all needed to be called down to be aware that there was a day of accountability a-coming. A day when we would stand before the judge. Some of the guys in my class had stood before a judge at the local court, but we had no concept of the threat of standing before the Eternal Judge described by the country preacher in his Annual End-of-the-World Sermon.

This experience, plus in-depth biblical and philosophical studies, leads me to go easy on the subject of the end-times in my thoughts and in my preaching. But I mention this now because I want to alert my younger friends to the fact that I MAY BE WRONG! I don't think I am. I believe that there will be a year 1999 and a year 2001 and so on, but I may be wrong. At any rate, I don't think you can afford to be apathetic about this business and risk your whole future life on just my opinion! It could be later than you think! I would suggest that you live as though I'm wrong and hope that I'm right!

Seriously, although you and I continue to live upon the earth, the lives of many of our loved ones have ended. The end of time as we know it has come for them. They have moved beyond the limits of clock and calendar. This year my father has moved beyond. Eighteen members of the church where I am pastor died during this past year. It is a sobering thought to wonder which of us will be among that number next year. But death is a part of life, you know. It will surely come knocking on our door. Sooner or later. We hope later rather than sooner, but it will come. And when Death arrives, it will be the end of time as we have known it.

But for those who have belief, who have eyes to see beyond the obvious, it is true that the end is but the beginning. My friend in the nursing home asked the question: "Is it the end or the beginning?"

And through a fleeting glance she answered her own question: "It is another new beginning."

Dietrich Bonhoeffer was executed on Sunday, April 9, 1945. His fellow prisoners in the Nazi concentration camp reported later that he had been leading a worship service. Just as he finished the last prayer, the door opened and two SS troopers pushed their way inside. One shouted, "Prisoner Bonhoeffer! Come with us!" The rest of the prisoners knew what it meant: Bonhoeffer was to be executed! As he walked out, he told his fellow prisoners, "This is the end. But for me, the beginning of life."

This is a statement that any of us can choose to make at the endings within our lives. To do so may take courage and dedication to new ways.

But know this: our God gives to us a whole series of new beginnings. Although they may look like endings, to those who have eyes to see they are truly opportunities for growth and opportunity. To become the person you want to be, seize these endings to make new beginnings.

This is a day of new beginnings,
time to remember and move on,
time to believe what love is bringing,
laying to rest the pain that's gone.

Then let us, with the Spirit's daring,
step from the past and leave behind
our disappointment, guilt, and grieving,
seeking new paths, and sure to find.

Christ is alive and goes before us
to show and share what love can do.
This is a day of new beginnings.
Our God is making all things new.

Brian Wren
Revelation 21:5

Afterword

Have you started yet to become a new you? Of course you have! Don't let the word "start" confuse you. You have already made choices, identified values, developed qualities and dreamed dreams that can change you for the better. If you have persisted in reading to the end of this book, you must have the desire! Most certainly, you have the perseverance!

Just as God's plan for little children allows them to progress: to sit and crawl, then pull up and stand—all before walking or running—God's plan for us is to grow spiritually in similar stages.

I believe, along with T. S. Eliot, that "to make an end is to make a beginning. The end is where we start from." As you put an end to each habit or attitude that hinders you, a beginning is waiting to happen.

Make it happen!
Let's begin!

NOTES

I gratefully acknowledge all the rich sources of data and inspiration which have come to me through the years, some of which I know and have quoted and cited in their proper places, and some which, though highly valuable, are unfortunately unlocatable.

[1] Thomas Cahill, *How the Irish Saved Civilization* (New York: Doubleday Anchor Books, 1995), p. 41.

[2] Edward C. Sellner, *Mentoring, The Ministry of Spiritual Kinship* (Notre Dame, Indiana: Ave Maria Press, 1990), pp. 17, 18.

[3] C. S. Lewis, *Screwtape Letters* as quoted in The Joyful Christian, Readings from C.S. Lewis (New York City: Macmillan Publishing Co., Inc., 1977), pp. 153, 154.

[4] Mother Teresa, *The Love of Christ* (New York City: Harper & Row, 1982), p. 112.

[5] William Bennett, *The Book of Virtues, A Treasury of Great Moral Stories* (New York City: Simon & Schuster, 1993)

[6] William H. Willimon and Stanley Hauerwas, *Resident Aliens* (Nashville: Abingdon Press, 1989), p. 49.

[7] Joyce M. Shutt, published in *The Mennonite* and quoted in Longacre, Doris Janzen, *Living More With Less* (Scottsdale, Pensylvania: Herald Press, 1980), p. 14.

[8] Shutt., p. 33.

[9] William James, quoted by Dorothy Day in *The Long Loneliness* (New York City: Harper and Row, 1952), pp. 118, 119.

[10] John H. Westerhoff, III, *A Pilgrim People* (Minneapolis: The Seabury Press, 1984), pp. 4,5.

[11] Oswald Chambers, *My Utmost for His Highest* (Grand Rapids, Michigan: Discovery House, 1935, 1963), p. 51.

[12] Patricia Wilson, *How Can I Be Over the Hill* (Nashville: Upper Room Books, 1989), p. 49.

[13] Clifford Irving, *Final Argument* (New York City: Dell Publishing Co., Inc., 1994), p. 152.

[14] Margaret Anne Huffman, from June Cotner, *Graces: Prayers and Poems for Everyday Meals and Special Occasions* (San Francisco: HarperSan Francisco 1994), p.7.

[15] Arthur Gordon, *A Touch of Wonder* (New York City: Guideposts Association, 1974), p. 111.

[16] Edward C. Sellner, *Mentoring, The Ministry of Spiritual Kinship* (Notre Dame, Indiana: Ave Maria Press, 1990) p. 147.

[17] Leonard Sweet, *The Jesus Prescription for a Healthy Life* (Nashville: Abingdon Press, 1996), p. 174.

[18] Sweet, p. 177.

[19] Barton Hunter, *The Big Difference* (St. Louis: Bethany Press, 1957), p. 14.

[20] Albert E. Cliff, *Lessons in Successful Living* (Englewood Cliffs, New Jersey: Prentice Hall, Inc., 1943), p. 43.